KU-011-323

PARENTING
GOD'S WAY

PARENTING GOD'S WAY

ALISTAIR BEGG

10 Publishing
a division of 10ofthose.com

Unless otherwise stated, Scripture quotations are taken from THE HOLY BIBLE, NEW INTERNATIONAL VERSION (Anglicised Edition). Copyright © 1973, 1979, 1984 by Biblica (formerly International Bible Society). Used by permission of Hodder & Stoughton Publishers. All rights reserved. 'NIV' is a registered trademark of Biblica. UK trademark number 1448790.

Copyright © 2017 by Alistair Begg
First published in Great Britain in 2017

The right of Alistair Begg to be identified as the Author of this Work has been asserted by him in accordance with the Copyright, Designs and Patents Act 1988.

All rights reserved. No part of this publication may be reproduced, stored in a retrieval system or transmitted in any form or by any means, electronic, mechanical, photocopying, recording or otherwise, without the prior permission of the publisher or the Copyright Licensing Agency.

British Library Cataloguing in Publication Data
A record for this book is available from the British Library

ISBN: 9781911272656

Typeset by: Pete Barnsley (CreativeHoot.com)
Printed in Denmark by Nørhaven

10Publishing, a division of 10ofthose.com
Unit C, Tomlinson Road, Leyland, PR25 2DY, England

Email: info@10ofthose.com
Website: www.10ofthose.com

INTRODUCTION

What is the greatest problem facing our nation? Is it the convoluted agenda of a political party, the threat of environmental catastrophe, or gathering storms on the international front? Is it the dire prophecies of Wall Street economists?

No. Most people today would agree that the most troubling road on which our country is traveling begins and ends at our own front doors. It's all in the family. For the last three decades, the idea of the traditional family has been under cultural assault. Every movement from the so-called sexual revolution to same-sex parenting has taken its toll on the foundational building blocks of our society. Now the social scientists realize that the damage has been significant. Families are reeling. Single parents struggle in the rubble of broken homes, and children come of age dizzily on the joint-custody merry-go-round.

Parents are sending distress signals. How can we save our homes? Does anyone know the answer?

Someone does. He has had the answer all along, and He is waiting for us to ask for it. We can find the redemptive, creative details lovingly recorded in an ancient book and fleshed out in the author's own Son. In God lies the perfect answer to parenting, for God the Father is the perfect parent.

Let's explore what He has to say first to fathers, then to mothers.

BEING A FATHER GOD'S WAY

Where Have All the Fathers Gone?

Men are masters of the art of delegation. Give them a task, and they can quickly assign just the right person to do it. A simple phone call? Let the office assistant make the connection. Household chore? One of the kids can get it done. Something in men gravitates toward a well-ordered corporate structure.

Yes, delegation is a wonderful thing, but what about abdication? What if we assign away our own responsibilities? Another word for that is abandonment, and that is largely the sad state of Christian fatherhood today. Fathers are meant to nurture and admonish their children in the Lord Jesus, but many delegating dads have abdicated that lofty seat of authority. Let Mom or the school or the church staff have the job. If all else fails, there is always the television set. Thus, we look up and down the pews and see wives, mothers, and single women in our churches – but few men. To offer a different spin to the Peter, Paul, and Mary song:[1] Where have all the fathers gone?

Paul on Parenting

In Ephesians 6:4, the Apostle Paul tells us where those fathers should be: "Fathers, do not exasperate your children; instead, bring them up in the training and instruction of the Lord." This exhortation is repeated in Colossians,[2] so we know it is particularly important. Fathers are to spend plenty of time with their children, training and instructing them. This time with their children simply cannot be delegated.

Just the same, modern men have tried to do so. In an age of career advancement and unprecedented leisure time, the daily task of fathering has struck too many men as unglamorous. They have left their work to others,

---

[1] Pete Seeger, "Where Have All the Flowers Gone," (1955).
[2] Colossians 3:21 (NIV).

and with these results: rising rates of suicide among minors, criminal activity and violence, drug abuse, and homosexuality. We have produced a floundering, confused, and self-destructive generation. This is no melodramatic overstatement, but the conclusion of any number of objective studies. There is no substitute for the work of the father in the home.

Authority: Abused versus Absent

So Paul, in Holy Scripture, pleads for fathers to rightfully give their children that time, and these words to the Ephesians were written in a context that would provide a striking contrast to the first-century world of Roman culture. The Roman father was an autocrat. He could order his children around as if they were cattle. The laws backed his ability to sell them as slaves if he so chose. He could even apply the death penalty in cases of extreme discipline.

Against that troubling backdrop, Paul presents a strikingly different parental perspective. He offers a radical suggestion that would cause first-century fathers to shine in a dark time, and it does the same in the twenty-first century. In our own world, the problem is not so much the abuse of authority as the absence of it.

Some throw up their hands in surrender. How can anyone know how to be a father without good models? "I can't be a good father, because, you see, I never had one myself." Or, "I need guidance to be a father in this modern world, but who has time to take a course or read a book?" Paul puts the lie to these excuses. The beauty of this principle is that no earthly model is necessary, whether from experience or curriculum. We could be surrounded with the most derelict of fathering role models, and we could still excel. For our model is God the Father Himself, as Paul established earlier, in Ephesians 3:14. Everyone shares a perfect heavenly Father, so everyone can be a good earthly one. Let's discover how we are to set out doing that.

Exasperation that Embitters

Paul begins with a negative command: Do not exasperate your children.[3] In other words, do not embitter or

---

[3] Ephesians 6:4.

provoke them. So far, so good; how many would admit to setting out each morning to provoke their children? But just the same, we do so without ever intending it. The heat of a million moments produces friction in many forms. The patterns of provocation intertwine; they grow as complex as the relationships themselves. Finally, father and child are mutually exasperated. Where did we go wrong?

Granted, laying down biblical principles will not keep everyone happy and hearty each moment of every day. As a matter of fact, the precepts of Christian parenting will provoke arguments and friction of their own. That's okay. We stand by the ways of truth even if we lose points in the home popularity game. Some exasperation simply comes with the territory.

But that is not the real problem, is it? We are more concerned with the frustration of our children that comes not from our wisest moments, but from those unwise things we say and do in our weaker moments. What is it that truly frustrates our children? What drives them to slowly smolder during their wonder years until they wonder if we love them?

Eight Exasperators

I can list eight sure-fire ways to exasperate my own children. Perhaps you have been there, too.

1. We exasperate them by failing to allow them to be themselves: children. We make demands or offer comments that fail to take into consideration their inexperience and immaturity. Sure, they can be silly. We can quickly point out all their fallacies because we are older and see the flaws, but they have a right to be children and to learn for themselves. To constantly draw attention to their immaturity is to slowly crush their spirits, undermine their confidence, and extinguish that lovely light that we call childlike. Let children have a childhood.

2. We exasperate them by treating them harshly and cruelly. Children are fragile. Whether physically or mentally, we can be overly forceful with them. A man may take pride in not being physically abusive, but what about verbal and emotional abuse? The tongue creates deeper wounds than the hand.

3. We exasperate by ridiculing them before others, particularly their peers. When our children's friends

are guests in our homes, perhaps we make a string of little remarks that seem inconsequential to us, but young ears hear them loud and clear. Young hearts store them, and exasperation builds.

4. We exasperate them by displaying favoritism and making unhelpful comparisons. All children are not the same. Qualities, abilities, and appearances are not the same. We exasperate our children when we play them against each other: "Why can't you clean your plate like your brother?" or "Why don't you apply yourself at school like your sister?"

5. We exasperate with our failure to express approval. Even in the little things, we sometimes withhold our blessings. It is all too easy. Perhaps we are absorbed in some television show, and our children bring us their drawings, craving a little credit and affirmation. "That's fine, that's lovely," we mumble as we try to move them from our line of vision. We care about our children, but at that moment they certainly do not feel it.

6. We exasperate them with the arbitrary exercise of discipline. Inconsistency breeds confusion in our children, who need to know exactly where they stand. Too often we issue discipline by mood swing, so that

one moment this behavior means early bedtime, and the next moment it is easily overlooked. We fail to realize we are arbitrary and capricious.

7. We exasperate them by neglecting them and treating them as intruders. They perceive that they are preempting our real concerns; they are somehow holding us back from what we would like to be doing. How must they feel to be treated as the chains that clamp us down? They are the most precious treasure in our arms, not the albatross around our necks.

8. Finally, we exasperate them by pushing them toward our goals rather than their own. If we are not careful, we'll confuse the two. How many of us drag our children to the little league field to introduce them to their destiny? Do we hear our own voices from the grandstand? We overlay our personal agendas without nurturing our children's desires.

Such are the ways we exasperate our children, but this list is not exhaustive: there are many others. We exasperate through smothering them with overprotection, by holding them in the nest. We can protect, yet provoke. We exasperate them by making our love conditional. We can be devilishly creative in the ways we fail God and His desire that we build strong children.

Paul's Positive Instruction

We have considered Paul's negative instruction concerning exasperation. The apostle dealt with the same idea in Colossians 3:21: "Fathers, do not embitter your children, or they will become discouraged." Discouragement is ultimately the fruit of all those little mistakes along the road of raising our children.

Now let us look at the positive side of Paul's teaching. The alternative, of course, to exasperating and discouraging a child is encouraging him. All parents aspire to this ideal. With patient and loving stimulation, gifts and potential will blossom and bear fruit.

This is the more positive idea to which Paul turns his attention in the second half of Ephesians 6:4. Do not discourage those children; "instead, bring them up in the training and instruction of the Lord." How is a father to do that?

The Care and Feeding of Children

Paul uses the phrase "bring them up." The Greek word

here is quite crucial. It means nourishing or feeding. Near this verse, in Ephesians 5:29, the same verb is used: "After all, no one ever hated his own body, but he feeds and cares for it …" The idea of nourishment is very important to Paul. We nurture and nourish our bodies and our children as Christ does the church.

So the duty of feeding and nurturing the child belongs to the father. This in no way demeans or diminishes the critical work of the mother, but the father is assigned by God the spiritual and emotional care and feeding of his children. How he feeds them, and what he feeds them, will be noted by the children. The food he considers nonessential will also be noted. For example, if the father continuously feeds and nurtures his children's mental development by reading books, asking questions, and spurring them to think, the children will strive to grow mentally.

What if the father only occasionally serves up the spiritual meal? What if the family's faith is little more than a between-meal snack, and what if the father then dishes it out to his children, but leaves his own plate empty? Children's big eyes miss nothing. They know ambivalence when they see it. If spirituality is not a particular priority in the balanced diet of a family, we cannot expect our children to gravitate toward spiritual values for sustenance as they begin to grow and reach out to feed themselves. The obsessions and priorities of the father will become the obsessions and priorities of his children, and in exactly the same way, those things he disregards and ignores will also be pushed away by his children.

Training and Instruction

Martyn Lloyd-Jones, writing on Ephesians 6, says this: "If parents but gave as much thought to the rearing of [their] children as they do to the rearing of animals and flowers, the situation would be very different."[4] We are what we eat, and they are what we feed them.

Alongside that idea of feeding and nourishing, Paul places two more key words. The first is "training." The best picture of that word's meaning can be found in Hebrews 12:10–11:

---

[4] David Martyn Lloyd-Jones, Life in the Spirit in Marriage, Home, and Work: An Exposition of Ephesians 5:18-69 (Edinburgh: Banner of Truth Trust, 1974), 290.

Our fathers disciplined us for a little while as they thought best; but God disciplines us for our good, that we may share in his holiness. No discipline seems pleasant at the time, but painful. Later on, however, it produces a harvest of righteousness and peace for those who have been trained by it.

This word "discipline" is the same one Paul uses, here translated as "training."

Children understand that "no discipline seems pleasant at the time." They have experienced a variety of unpleasant forms of discipline, but children always miss the double meaning here: The discipline can be unpleasant for the one who disciplines, too. Few things are as unpleasant to parents as applying punishment to their children, and nothing is easier than to take the easy way out and forego discipline. As parents, we would love to take the path of least resistance and neglect discipline, simply overlooking an incident.

The Wisdom of Discipline

Paul says this responsibility cannot be evaded, not if we are going to raise wise, strong, healthy children in Christ. Training, if it is to have integrity and be effective, always involves rules, regulations, rewards, and punishments. It is the training Solomon describes repeatedly in Proverbs, notably Proverbs 13:24: "He who spares the rod hates his son, but he who loves him is careful to discipline him." Love means discipline, and Proverbs 22:15: "Folly is bound up in the heart of a child, but the rod of discipline will drive it far from him."

This is a critical issue for all families, and our tendency is to come down on one of the two opposite sides. We become extremists, whether it is in excessive, heavy-handed strictness or lenient laxity.

Sometimes parents simply must punish, but sometimes we should never punish, such as when we are annoyed, our pride is hurt, or we have lost our temper. Easier said than done! Many of us, if pressed, might admit that when we do punish, it is invariably under one of those three conditions. We become increasingly annoyed with our children's behavior, and our feelings build until we strike out at them under the guise of discipline. The punishment serves more as an outlet for our feelings than a corrective to the child.

When we do make this common but damaging mistake, it is important that we find our children before bedtime, draw them close to us, and express our apologies. We should always be able to apologize to our children. Too many kids grow up with a father who could never say the words, "I'm sorry."

The Avoidance of Discipline

Discipline must be of the right kind. There must be appropriate rewards and punishments, rules and regulations. We must avoid the two traps, the first being a heavy-handed reign of fear in our households, and the second being the forfeiture of accountability. Some fathers leave that responsibility to their wives or a teacher or no one at all. As damaging as overzealous discipline might be, lax discipline is just as destructive.

The Wisdom of Instruction

If "training" is what we do with the child, then Paul's second word has to do with what we say. This is the word "instruction." It means laying down principles that a child's mind can understand, framing their tiny lives with boundaries and standards.

Along the highway of growing up, our children will test every rule and press against the constraints of every boundary. We know this not merely from our experience as parents, but as former children. We push the edges to know where the boundaries are and to discover if there is a limit to our father's love. As we grow older, we begin to respect his ability to say "no." We begin to associate that word with love; this, of course, is the beginning of wisdom.

God gives fathers the responsibility of instruction. Sunday school instruction is a wonderful thing. Instruction at godly Christian schools is beneficial too, but ultimately, the issue of guidance boils down to the father; his training and instruction will make or break the child. If his instruction is godly and complete, the result is a well-rounded child of strong enough character and sufficiently stern moral fiber to weather any of life's storms. In its absence, the result is a confused human being who begins life with two strikes against him. Dads, your children look first to you.

Invading the Mind

Does a father's godly training and instruction mean he is "invading the child's mind?" Is this some violation of a spiritual bill of rights? Many trendy soothsayers would tell you so. From all the accumulated wisdom of nondirective counseling and client-centered therapy, they insist that it is not for the parents to inscribe a single chalk mark on the empty slate that is a young mind. Invariably the context of this advice, of course, is none other than religious training. Presumably, parents trample on their children's God-given right to reject God when they impose their adult spiritual views.

Obviously, this is patent hogwash, just as it has always been. Children need to have their minds invaded. So do adults, for that matter. We are hopelessly doomed without the godly invasion of Jesus Christ, the Word of God incarnate. Children need not indoctrination, but stimulation. We need to instill in them our own excitement for the things of God. They are naturally fascinated by the issues that fascinate us. The only deprivation of freedom that we need ever worry about is the lack of information necessary for our children to make the right choices. They crave the guidelines, framework, and absolutes of the kingdom of God. To deprive them of those is to tell them that we do not care.

Seeds of Destruction

Now it must be stated that children need just enough "wiggle room" to wrestle with the issues for themselves. We err by shoveling in the doctrine passionately, without giving it time to settle. Even the good gardener allows for the sun, the right fertilizer, and regular watering. The dinner table should be a place where questions can be asked and doubts expressed; children must have the opportunity to make their beliefs their own as they work out their faith with fear and trembling. Not indoctrination, but stimulation.

Of the Lord

The last three words of Paul should not be passed over easily: "of the Lord." These serve as more than simply punctuation for a sentence. These three words, taken together, are the last word. For when all is said and done, all of our training must be "in the Lord"; all of our instruction must be in the Lord. If we are to ultimately prevail in this grand challenge of parenting, we ourselves must be in the Lord.

We will teach our children many things, from baseball to baking and from fishing to fashion. Our lessons will range from the sublime to the ridiculous, but underlining all is the lordship of Christ. That is the foundation of the learning experience, no matter what the building blocks may be. You are the teacher, but Christ is always the principal. When we exercise discipline, it is essentially God's discipline; when we smile with pride and pleasure at the progress of our offspring, we know that God smiles with us – a father and a Father, sharing a child.

The final, ultimate lesson we seek to teach is the story of a child's heart coming together with Christ's heart. If we fail to teach that lesson, then all our instruction has been in vain. It is the only question on the final examination of our parenting. Are we studying for that examination? Do we make as much effort to read the Scriptures with our children as we make to attend their swim meets? Do we emphasize family devotionals the way we emphasize their school work? All of those things, no matter how important they are now, will one day fade; what must remain is the heart of your child, offered wholly to the heart of Christ.

BEING A MOTHER GOD'S WAY

The Sacred Duty of Motherhood

We have seen that God ordains fathers to train and instruct their children in the Lord and to avoid exasperating them. We have noted that too many fathers abdicate this task, when it is their duty alone, and we have reflected on some of the dreadful implications of that abdication.

Where does this leave mothers? Are they relegated to a position of assistant parent, summoned occasionally from the family bullpen for relief work whenever the father is tired or indisposed? Does the Bible somehow marginalize the place of motherhood in bringing up a child?

Not in the least! We will find that motherhood is, in every sense, the sacred institution established specially by God that fatherhood is. The role may be different, but it is never inferior.

Ask any American. In our country, Mother's Day is a far more profitable day in the greeting card industry than Father's Day. More than one hundred years ago, just before the outbreak of World War I, Congress passed a resolution to honor mothers on the second Sunday in May. President Woodrow Wilson also called on the public to display their flags as an expression of "our love and reverence for the mothers of our country,"[5] and so it has been ever since.

Yet today, after one hundred years of reverence for the unique and sacred institution that is motherhood, the U.S. Congress is now busy with resolutions that would just as uniquely damage the position of mothers in America.

A rabid political agenda is determined to legally establish that anyone can be a mother, regardless of

---

[5] Woodrow Wilson, "Mother's Day Proclamation of May 9, 1914, Proclamation 1268," General Records of the United States Government, 1778–1992 (May 5, 1914): National Archives, Record Group 11, http://bit.ly/2qmXoC0 (accessed March 23, 2017).

gender, sexual orientation, or biological relationship. The real mothers, those who have borne the load since creation, are being challenged. Thus it is all the more crucial, in the present political climate, that we come to understand what God says about motherhood. We must hear the message clearly.

We will discover that the Bible clearly affirms the family as the foundational unit of society, that parents are worthy of the highest honor on earth, and that mothers are entrusted by God with a sacred duty, which is theirs and theirs alone.

Can Anyone Be a Mother?

These new "experts" bring the message that anyone is qualified to be a mother, but the position of Scripture on that issue is quite different indeed. God has a very special place for mothers in His created order. They are among His most sacred and beautiful gifts to humanity.

However, mothers do not always feel like sacred and beautiful gifts to humanity. Their daily work does not always carry a glorious sheen about it. On any given day, there are lunches and laundry, maid service and taxi service – all of it taken for granted by the permanent guests of the Mom Hotel. As those bright blurs, better known as her children, whiz past occasionally with open hands, and she follows behind with the vacuum cleaner, wearing a deep path in the carpet between here and the washing machine, Mother feels significantly less than special.

"Sacred privilege" is not the phrase which comes first to mind when she pulls herself from her bed early on an overcast Monday morning. No, "privilege" would mean being able to wake up in her own way, rather than opening her heavy eyelids to the sight of the children lined up by the side of the bed with frozen stares and a list of requests. There is Christmas tinsel growing from the carpet, the arms of the sofa are worn through, the refrigerator is empty, there are no clean diapers, and some unidentified finger has scrawled "Go Bulls" in the dust on the coffee table.

And they want us to believe anyone can be a mother? Those lobbyists may have spent plenty of time in Washington, but they have obviously spent little in a home.

A Culture Confused

In truth, Mother is not the one who is confused; she is only tired. Our culture, however, is filled with confusion on the role of motherhood. Movies have forwarded the agenda that somehow, after thousands of years, the job qualifications are being expanded to include anyone who applies.

We are now to believe that gender is not particularly important in mothering. "Why," they say, "any person in any context at any particular time and in any living environment can be a mother." On the face of it, they choose to ignore a few inflexible physiological realities. Only the mother's body, for example, produces the necessary nourishment for the infant's life in those early weeks and months, but the progressive crowd dismisses that as a mere mistake of the evolutionary process, rather than a logical part in the harmony of the Creator's beautiful plan. From the creation of the world, God established a unique role for the man and a unique role for the woman.

The feminist agenda is unhappy with the traditional institution of motherhood. Susan Faludi, best-selling feminist author, writes that we are victims of our chromosomes and hormones; that women are too deferential to male authority, too needful of male validation, and too subject to innuendo and misrepresentation to resist exploitation. Women must, therefore, claw their way to the top where they belong. So, accepting anything short of what we know we deserve and all that men owe us signals betrayal, she proclaims. Further, according to Faludi, to compromise is to contribute to what she sees as an antifeminist backlash; it is to undo thirty-five years of struggle. Women are not permitted the option of accommodating anyone else's agenda but their own.[6]

Thus, one author calls women into an aggressive war against men, tradition, the home, and, ultimately – make no mistake – God, for His agenda most surely conflicts with this feminist one of coming out on top.

Clarity for the Confusion

The church must speak out in a clear, unified voice that the liberation promised for women leads only to

---

[6] Susan Faludi, Backlash: The Undeclared War Against American Women (New York: Doubleday, 1991).

deeper bondage. For the only freedom available is the kind available when the truth, as Jesus promised, sets us free.[7] That truth is found in the Bible, in every detail of how our lives are to be lived, and that includes the details of motherhood. The clarity of Scripture is more than a match for the confusion of our culture.

One of the greatest misconceptions about the New Testament is the myth that it somehow denigrates women. Just the reverse is true. The broad sweep of Scripture reveals quite a liberating role for women, from the Garden of Eden to the ministry of Jesus and beyond. It is a historical fact that women were harshly repressed in the New Testament world in which Jesus appeared. They were treated as little more than the private property of their husbands. The new life of the Gospel, as expressed by the epistles, offered women full citizenship in the kingdom of God. Whereas the Jewish synagogue had been a men-only affair, the new churches, usually meeting in synagogues, were open to women. In contrast to Greek, Roman, and Jewish cultures, it was only the radical new faith of Christianity that recognized full human rights for

---

[7] John 8:32.

women. When Paul wrote in Galatians 3 that in Christ there is "neither male nor female,"[8] he was writing words that, to most of the world, seemed insane.

The Older Women

Paul, in his letter to Titus, offers us a window into the place of women in the first-century church: "Then they can train the younger women to love their husbands and children, to be self-controlled and pure, to be busy at home, to be kind, and to be subject to their husbands, so that no one will malign the word of God."[9]

Paul is speaking, obviously, of older women and their special ministry. These women have the advantage of their years of experience. They have the opportunity to offer the value of their accumulated years to the younger mothers, who are establishing their homes for the first time.

An observer of Christian missions in India was asked what the greatest need of the church was there. E. F. Brown answered unequivocally that the greatest

---

[8] Galatians 3:28.
[9] Titus 2:4–5 (NIV).

need was godly grandmothers "who have lived out the principles of the Book, who have reared their families, who have known a measure of success, having faced the challenges and the disappointments and the failures, and who then are able to provide the instruction necessary for young women living in a confused culture and looking for clarity from the Bible."[10] It is no different in any culture. The younger generation desperately needs to hear the stories of those who have gone before.

The Privilege of Motherhood

Notice the spontaneity by which the women in Paul's reference are working together. They are creating an impact through informal contact. For most of us, the learning that really lingers throughout life is received this way – not in rigid notetaking in classes or organized groups. Those who have influenced us most have done so quietly in the daily give-and-take of life. Amid the confusion and chaos of modern culture, today's young mothers need their elder sisters.

---

[10] William Barclay, The Letters to Timothy, Titus, and Philemon (Philadelphia: Westminster, 1960), 248.

Every mother is involved in the awesome task of building a home. There is no more incredible privilege in this life. However strong the pangs of childbirth, they are nothing to the pangs in her heart as she watches her children grow and prepares them to leave home and build their own. She presides over the forging of young personalities. She converts ancient Christian principles to budding character in the lives of her offspring. She labors in a laboratory whose results may not become evident for fifteen or twenty years, after which the physical, emotional, social, and spiritual aspects she has molded will reveal the strong human beings she has helped to craft. The mother knows she is about the great, ultimate work of her life.

Again, we hear the dissonant voice of our culture: "Home," it says to women, "is your prison! Liberate yourself in the job market!" That is the true privilege, says our culture: drawing a bimonthly paycheck. Why should you stay home and work sixteen hours a day without pay?

Real-life mothers are beginning to question that "wisdom." After a few years in the jungle of jobs, USA, they begin to understand that to "stay home" is a privilege. Pay? What better pay is there than the lives of one's children? They are far better than gold.

The Priorities of Motherhood : Love

Motherhood, then, is a privilege, and it establishes the priorities of a woman's life. Paul's Titus passage reveals four key priorities for mothers.

Mothers are to be taught, first, to love their husbands and children. Ephesians 5 tells us that husbands are to love their wives,[11] and here we find the reverse as an instruction.

Shouldn't some things come naturally? Must we be taught how to love? Our culture tells us all the time, through popular songs and movies, that love is simply an emotion. One song says: "What's love got to do with it? What's love but a second hand emotion?"[12] That is a starkly different definition from the scriptural one! The Bible tells us that "the greatest of these is love,"[13] and it

---

[11] Ephesians 5:25.
[12] Terry Britten and Graham Lyle, "What's Love Got to Do with It" (1984); recorded by Tina Turner and others.
[13] 1 Corinthians 13:13.

remains when nearly all else passes away; if we have not love, we are nothing.[14] We must indeed be taught to love our husbands, wives, and children.

The Bible teaches us how to love as God intends. It also teaches that when that kind of love is missing, nothing else can fill the gap. If a wife cannot love her family as God intends, no career success will make up the difference. No expensive home will do. Yet conversely, godly love will pull us through when careers are in jeopardy and when the roof falls in. Mothers should immerse themselves in Scripture and learn to love.

Self-Control and Purity

What else is a priority for wives, according to the epistle to Titus? They should not only know how to love their husbands and children, but they must have self-control and purity. These are requirements for all Christians, but particularly those in leadership. Ask mothers themselves and they will tell you that in every area of motherhood, self-control is required: time,

---

[14] 1 Corinthians 13:2.

home management, caring for children, and so on. They must keep in good health. They must watch their tempers in the stress of caring for children. All these things take self-control.

Mothers must also be pure in an adulterous generation. They must have surpassing loyalty to their husband and children. The priority of family must be unchallenged, and that means purity.

Busy at Home, and Kind

Next, our passage tells us of the priorities of being busy at home and maintaining kindness. Our culture would like to blot out the female imperative of being occupied with the home. Women should "have it all," shouldn't they? They should have all kinds of extracurricular activities, according to the world's wisdom, but the fact remains that no greater contribution to society can be made than to labor in the maintenance of a godly home. All of our strength as a nation proceeds from the integrity of our individual homes, from which our children emerge to further the next generation. Doing all that is necessary in that home will keep any woman busy – again, ask any mother.

Because our society is filled with single mothers, this is not always possible. Most single mothers do not glory in their career opportunities. They would love the freedom to build a home for their children during the day. This dilemma underscores the truth of the Scriptures: our culture's shining ideal of the working mother is fool's gold. Mothers busy building their homes are also busy building a stronger society. They who labor in the workplace strengthen a company, but they who labor in the home build the future.

But why is kindness mentioned here? This time, ask the husbands. At some point, they have been charged with taking care of things while their wives were away. Within mere minutes, the house was in chaos! Where are things kept? How does the vacuum cleaner work? How does one handle this situation? Husbands will reveal that they came away with a profound respect for their wives, particularly in the matter of remaining kind amid the chaos of home maintenance! One of the greatest manifestations of the woman's grace is that, under fire, she can maintain a pleasing countenance.

Subject to Their Husbands

Fourth, wives are to be subject to their husbands. We cannot live as God intends without faithfulness to this principle. When wives fail in this area, a domino effect comes into play, and every other aspect of the home is adversely affected. It is simply part of God's arrangement for things. Of course we must understand the wonder of our equality before God, as set out in Galatians 3, but that equality does not negate God's ordinance by which father and husband shall be the spiritual leader in the home, and wife and mother shall submit to that headship.

Yes, it sounds backward in our modern world. Much of the way in which we live our lives today can be compared to a journey in which we find ourselves lost. We are certain we have followed the directions precisely, yet here we are wandering without a clue. Backtracking, we find that someone has turned the signpost around at an intersection, and we took the wrong way without realizing it. That is the challenge confronting today's wives and mothers as they make the journey of building Christian homes: The world has turned the signposts around.

The Potential of Motherhood

We have examined the privilege of being a mother. We have taken a look at four priorities given by Scripture. What of the potential? At the end of Titus 2:5, Paul says that if we can do all these things, the Word of God will not be maligned by people.

The reason for this is simple: We are the only Bible many people will read. They may have Bibles collecting dust on their shelves, but they never open them. They pay no attention to sermons or television preachers.

Those of us who live in submission to the wisdom of Scripture are the Word in flesh to such people. As long as we profess to be Christians, yet live no differently than the pagans surrounding us, those pagans can malign the Word; they can speak of "all the hypocrites in the church." They can dismiss the Bible as a sentimental piece of Victorian nostalgia, but when we follow the dictates of God's wisdom – building strong homes and presenting powerful examples of marriage and parenthood – something happens. People gape in wonder. They marvel at the difference between our lives and their own, and the respect they have for us transfers to respect for God's Word.

An Extraordinary Opportunity

Surely one of the greatest avenues for the impact of the Gospel, given the state of our culture, is motherhood. Crime rises with a new generation of young lawbreakers; drugs, suicide, and violence are becoming increasingly common among adolescents and preadolescents. More than fifty percent of our homes will be broken ones. In the face of all this, motherhood will become a greater focal point than ever. Then the world will see the image of the Christian home. That picture will speak more powerfully than thousands of words. All the cultural assumptions and trendy ideas of progress will quickly fade before the living truth of a home as God designed it. Whether they are ridiculed, whether the daytime talk shows endorse their lives, these mothers will love their husbands and children, practice self-control and purity, busy themselves in home-building, lovingly submit to their husbands, and all the while, remain kind so that the world will stammer, "That cannot be done under human power. What is her secret?"

That family on your street, the John Does, has no idea that the Bible offers any help whatsoever in child-rearing. They have been led to believe the Bible is strictly an anachronism, and now they are calling on you, in the midst of some crisis, as their home comes apart at the seams. It may be substance abuse or a runaway teen or pregnancy. It may be something else. In any case, there was nowhere else to turn, and in sheer desperation they thought of you after watching your family for years – the lovely manners and dispositions of your children, the happiness of your marriage, the way your family has flourished in a neighborhood where divorce and delinquency seem to rule the day – and on the phone, Mrs. Doe asks, "Where can I find some answers? Is there a book?"

Strength for the Battlefield

You can tell her, "Yes, there is a book!" When you suggest she may already have heard of it – might even own a copy – she is not likely to malign the Word, for you and your ways have earned the right to her respect. It isn't that your family is perfect – not by a long shot! We are honest enough to admit our failures. We affirm our struggles, but we can tell the Does, "Families are a battle. We all have our share of daily casualties. There are times when one wants to retreat or surrender, but we have a banner that flies over us at all times. We look to that flag, and it gives us strength. Not only that, but we never skirmish without direction. We have the greatest battle plan ever devised, and when one of us is wounded, we have the finest medicine and the greatest hospital. You see, the banner is God's love; the battle plan is God's Word; the hospital is His Church. And with all this support, your own family can be just as strong."

Loving Mothers, Loving God

Mothers are one of the greatest signposts God ever fixed on this earth. Somehow, they carry on daily with strength, love, consistency, the healing art, and just the right word at just the right time. When they pass on, things are never the same. The amazing care and effectiveness she displays in thousands of ways tells us that, behind them, there is a God who also cares. And in ways that even the best of mothers cannot reach us, cannot heal us, cannot offer the right word, there is someone even stronger, someone more perfect and availing. Loving mothers point us to a loving God.

And fathers? The greatest thing any father can do is to love his children's mother. The best gift he can give his children is to nurture her. As she pours herself out in the service of her offspring, the father and husband must do the same in caring for her.

This business of parenting, you see, is not for the timid. It is not for the weekend hobbyist. It cannot be "phoned in." It will take everything you have and everything you are, but that is only natural, for it involves everything God ever meant you to be. It is life's grand adventure. For the astounding mission ahead, God is looking for a few good men and women. Brace yourselves! There will be days when you grope for answers; you will have only God's Word, His love, and each other to hang onto. Expect a few bumps in the road. Tears will not be absent, but many of those tears will be happy ones, for when all is said and done, the pain will be nearly insignificant except for the way it helped you grow.

Your children will become adults and they will honor you. They will look to your example for guidance in becoming parents themselves. They will fill your arms with grandchildren. And as you grow older and gather to you the loving partner of your youth, there will be joy in seeing Christ – the same yesterday, today, and forever – still at work in a new generation. You can have the quiet joy of knowing that through the family you helped build, you have left the world a little better than you found it.

May God fill and bless your days as you take up the joy of parenting – His way.

10 Publishing
a division of 10ofthose.com

10Publishing is the publishing house of **10ofThose**. It is committed to producing quality Christian resources that are biblical and accessible.

www.10ofthose.com is our online retail arm selling thousands of quality books at discounted prices.

For information contact: **info@10ofthose.com**
or check out our website: **www.10ofthose.com**